This marriage study series is pure Focus on the Family—
reliable, biblically sound and dedicated to reestablishing family values
in today's society. This series will no doubt help a multitude of couples
strengthen their relationship, not only with each other,
but also with God, the *creator* of marriage itself.

Bruce Wilkinson
Author, The BreakThrough Series: *The Prayer of Jabez,*
Secrets of the Vine and *A Life God Rewards*

In this era of such need, Dr. Dobson's team has produced solid,
helpful materials about Christian marriage. Even if they have been
through marriage studies before, every couple—married or engaged—
will benefit from this foundational study of life together. Thanks to
Focus on the Family for helping set us straight in this top priority.

Charles W. Colson
Chairman, Prison Fellowship Ministries

In my 31 years as a pastor, I've officiated at hundreds of weddings.
Unfortunately, many of those unions failed. I only wish the *Focus on the*
Family Marriage Series had been available to me during those years.
What a marvelous tool you as pastors and Christian leaders have
at your disposal. I encourage you to use it to assist those you
serve in building successful, healthy marriages.

H. B. London, Jr.
Vice President, Ministry Outreach/Pastoral Ministries
Focus on the Family

Looking for a prescription for a better marriage?
You'll enjoy this timely and practical series!

Dr. Kevin Leman

Author, *Sheet Music: Uncovering the Secrets of*
Sexual Intimacy in Marriage

The *Focus on the Family Marriage Series* is successful because it shifts
the focus from how to fix or strengthen a marriage to *who* can do it.
Through this study you will learn that a blessed marriage will be the
happy by-product of a closer relationship with the *creator* of marriage.

Lisa Whelchel

Author, *Creative Correction* and
The Facts of Life and Other Lessons My Father Taught Me

In a day and age where the covenant of marriage is so quickly tossed
aside in the name of incompatibility and irreconcilable differences, a
marriage Bible study that is both inspirational and practical is desperately
needed. The *Focus on the Family Marriage Series* is what couples are seeking.
I give my highest recommendation to this Bible study series that has the
potential to dramatically impact and improve marriages today. Marriage
is not so much about finding the right partner as it is about being the
right partner. These studies give wonderful biblical teachings for
helping those who want to learn the beautiful art of being and
becoming all that God intends in their marriage.

Lysa TerKeurst

President, Proverbs 31 Ministries
Author, *Capture His Heart* and *Capture Her Heart*

focus on the family® marriage series

the
fighting
marriage

Gospel Light

Gospel Light is a Christian publisher dedicated to serving the local church. We believe God's vision for Gospel Light is to provide church leaders with biblical, user-friendly materials that will help them evangelize, disciple and minister to children, youth and families.

It is our prayer that this Gospel Light resource will help you discover biblical truth for your own life and help you minister to others. May God richly bless you.

For a free catalog of resources from Gospel Light, please call your Christian supplier or contact us at 1-800-4-GOSPEL *or* www.gospellight.com

PUBLISHING STAFF
William T. Greig, Chairman
Kyle Duncan, Publisher
Dr. Elmer L. Towns, Senior Consulting Publisher
Pam Weston, Senior Editor
Patti Pennington Virtue, Associate Editor
Hilary Young, Editorial Assistant
Jessie Minassian, Editorial Assistant
Bayard Taylor, M.Div., Senior Editor, Biblical and Theological Issues
Samantha A. Hsu, Cover and Internal Designer
Amy Simpson, Contributing Writer

ISBN 0-8307-3149-0
© 2003 Focus on the Family
All rights reserved.
Printed in the U.S.A.

table of contents

foreword

The most urgent mission field on Earth is not across the sea or even across the street—it's right where you live: in your home and family. Jesus' last instruction was to "make disciples of all nations" (Matthew 28:19). At the thought of this command, our eyes look across the world for our work field. That's not bad; it's just not *all*. God intended the home to be the first place of Christian discipleship and growth (see Deuteronomy 6:4-8). Our family members must be the *first* ones we reach out to in word and example with the gospel of the Lord Jesus Christ, and the fundamental way in which this occurs is through the marriage relationship.

Divorce, blended families, the breakdown of communication and the complexities of daily life are taking a devastating toll on the God-ordained institutions of marriage and family. We do not need to look hard or search far for evidence that even Christian marriages and families are also in a desperate state. In response to the need to build strong Christ-centered marriages and families, this series was developed.

Focus on the Family is well known and respected worldwide for its stead-fast dedication to preserving the sanctity of marriage and family life. I can think of no better partnership than the one formed by Focus on the Family and Gospel Light to produce the *Focus on the Family Marriage Series*. This series is well-written, biblically sound and right on target for guiding couples to explore the foundation God has laid for marriage and to see Him as the role model for the perfect spouse. Through these studies, seeds will be planted that will germinate in your heart and mind for many years to come.

In our practical, bottom-line culture, we often want to jump over the *why* and get straight to the *what*. We think that by *doing* the six steps or *learning* the five ways, we will reach the goal. But deep-rooted growth is slower and more purposeful and begins with a well-grounded understanding of God's divine design. Knowing why marriage exists is crucial to making the how-tos more effective. Marriage is a gift from God, a unique and distinct covenant relationship through which His glory and goodness can resonate, and it is only through knowing the architect and His plan that we will build our marriage on the surest foundation.

God created marriage; He has a specific purpose for it, and He is committed to filling with fresh life and renewed strength each union yielded to Him. God wants to gather the hearts of every couple together, unite them in love and walk them to the finish line—all in His great grace and goodness.

May God, in His grace, lead you into His truth, strengthening your lives and your marriage.

Gary T. Smalley
Founder and Chairman of the Board
Smalley Relationship Center

introduction

At the beginning of creation God "made them male and female." "For this reason a man will leave his father and mother and be united to his wife, and the two will become one flesh." So they are no longer two, but one.
Mark 10:6-8

The Fighting Marriage can be used in a variety of situations, including small-group Bible studies, Sunday School classes or counseling or mentoring situations. An individual couple can also use this book as an at-home marriage-building study.

Each of the four sessions contains four main components.

Session Overview

Tilling the Ground
This is an introduction to the topic being discussed—commentary and questions to direct your thoughts toward the main idea of the session.

Planting the Seed
This is the Bible study portion in which you will read Scripture and answer questions to help discover lasting truths from God's Word.

Watering the Hope
This is a time for discussion and prayer. Whether you are using the study at home as a couple, in a small group or in a classroom setting, talking about the lesson with your spouse is a great way to solidify the truth and plant it deeply into your hearts.

Harvesting the Fruit
As a point of action, this portion of the session offers suggestions on putting the truth of the Word into action in your marriage relationship.

Suggestions for Individual Couple Study

There are at least three options for using this study as a couple.

- It may be used as a devotional study that each spouse would study individually through the week; then on a specified day, come together and discuss what you have learned and how to apply it to your marriage.
- You might choose to study one session together in an evening and then work on the application activities during the rest of the week.
- Because of the short length of this study, it is a great resource for a weekend retreat. Take a trip away for the weekend, and study each session together, interspersed with your favorite leisure activities.

Suggestions for Group Study

There are many ways that this study can be used in a group situation. The most common way is in a small-group Bible study format. However, it can also be used in adult Sunday School class. However you choose to use it, there are some general guidelines to follow for group study.

- Keep the group small—five to six couples is probably the maximum.
- Ask couples to commit to regular attendance for the four weeks of the study. Regular attendance is a key to building relationships and trust in a group.
- Encourage participants *not* to share anything of a personal or potentially embarrassing nature without first asking the spouse's permission.
- Whatever is discussed in the group meetings is to be held in strictest confidence among group members only.

There are additional leader helps in the back of this book and in *The Focus on the Family Marriage Ministry Guide*.

Suggestions for Mentoring or Counseling Relationships

This study also lends itself for use in relationships where one couple mentors or counsels another couple.

- A mentoring relationship, where a couple that has been married for several years is assigned to meet on a regular basis with a younger couple, could be arranged through a system set up by a church or ministry.
- A less formal way to start a mentoring relationship is for a younger couple to take the initiative and approach a couple that exemplify a mature, godly marriage and ask them to meet with them on a regular basis. Or the reverse might be a mature couple that approaches a younger couple to begin a mentoring relationship.
- When asked to mentor, some might shy away and think that they could never do that, knowing that their own marriage is less than perfect. But just as we are to disciple new believers, we must learn to disciple married couples to strengthen marriages in this difficult world. The Lord has promised to be "with you always" (Matthew 28:20).
- Before you begin to mentor a couple, first complete the study yourselves. This will serve to strengthen your own marriage and prepare you for leading another couple.
- Be prepared to learn as much or more than the couple(s) you will mentor.

There are additional helps for mentoring relationships in *The Focus on the Family Marriage Ministry Guide.*

The Focus on the Family Marriage Series *is based on Al Janssen's* The Marriage Masterpiece *(Wheaton, IL: Tyndale House Publishers, 2001), an insightful look at what marriage can—and should—be. In this study, we are pleased to lead you through the wonderful journey of discovering the joy in your marriage that God wants you to experience!*

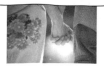

the causes of conflict

Do not worship any other god, for the LORD, whose name is Jealous, is a jealous God.
Exodus 34:14

What images come to mind when you hear the word "jealousy"? Do you envision flying pottery, stomping feet or slamming doors? Jealousy is so full of passionate emotion that it often cannot be expressed in words. Can you picture God being jealous?

The Lord is passionate toward His people. The Bible describes how God was angry when His love was spurned (see 1 Kings 11:9), was jealous when His nation was seduced by other lovers (see Ezekiel 16:36-37) and felt jilted when His people actively chose to follow "worthless idols" (Jeremiah 2:5).

When we think about how we've been hurt in our relationships, we recognize emotions similar to those God displayed in His indictment of Israel. Consumed with uncontrollable passion and rage, we often lash out in anger at our spouse. What causes these episodes of jealousy and anger? Most often, it is not one thing; it's a myriad of conflicts we entertain in our daily lives.

Whatever the causes may be, God wants you to identify the problem areas so that your relationship with your spouse *and* your relationship with God can continue to grow and mature.

tilling the ground

We live in a world filled with conflict. A cynical boss, a whining child, pressures from our spouse, a to-do list that never gets finished—there are many possible daily stresses that add tremendous pressure to marriages. It is no wonder that couples encounter conflict regularly.

1. What do you think are the most common sources of conflict in marriages? List at least four.

2. What particular issue(s) regularly triggers disagreement between you and your spouse?

3. What is one conflict that you and your spouse have resolved successfully?

Once we recognize the potential triggers for conflict, the next step—and often the most difficult—is to admit and deal with the conflicts between us and our spouse. This is essential to handling conflict in a constructive manner rather than a destructive one.

Conflict between God and Israel arose when they rebelled against Him. God had high expectations for His people, entrusting them with His blessed land and uniting Himself to them under a new covenant of grace (see Hosea 2:19-20). However, Israel still turned from the Lord in order to fulfill her own selfish desires.

4. According to Jeremiah 2:1-8, how did Israel forsake God?

    In what ways did God provide for His people before they turned from Him?

5. As you reread the passage, what emotion was God expressing toward Israel?

Conflict emerged between God and Israel because the people chose to follow other gods, even after God provided her with "a fertile land . . . and rich produce" (Jeremiah 2:7). Since God was the husband to His people, Israel, their forsaking of God for false idols was the same as if they had committed adultery. This stirred anger and jealousy in God's heart.

6. In Jeremiah 2:31-35, what three statements did the people say to further intensify God's anger?

What common attitudes permeate these three statements?

7. How might these attitudes be manifested and cause conflict in marriage?

Conflict escalates when antagonistic and negative attitudes strangle a relationship. It is important to discover exactly what stirs anger and jealousy in our hearts. Let's take a look at how Israel began cutting away at the roots of her relationship with God.

8. According to Jeremiah 3:21-25, what did the people of Israel recognize in themselves as a root conflict that hindered the unity between them and God?

What emotions filled the people as they recognized their wrongdoing and admitted their sin (v. 25)?

9. What did God say to His people before they confessed their sin?

Yes, Israel did indeed recognize the root cause of her conflict with the Lord. The people had turned away from God, who had loved, cared for and protected them; and they had turned toward worthless idols. Ironically, worshiping these idols did not make the people more joyful or satisfied in life.

It can be easy to believe that earthly possessions and other relationships will satisfy the longing in our souls. But without the Holy Spirit fulfilling our deepest human longings for relationship with God, all other means of filling the spiritual emptiness in us will fall short. No amount of earthly possessions or even human relationships can make up for the absence of God in a person's life.

Root Causes

From the Scriptures, we can identify two root causes that explain much of the strife between God and Israel.

Unrealized Expectations

God had grand expectations for Israel, expecting her to possess the fertile land and eat "its fruit and rich produce" (Jeremiah 2:7)—blessings that He had bestowed on her. When Israel received the gift but defiled the land and turned from God, His expectations were shattered.

10. According to Jeremiah 3:19, how did God treat His people?

11. What was God glad to bestow upon His people?

12. What did God expect His people to call Him and how did He expect them to respond to His graciousness?

From this brief yet poignant glance into God's character, we can see His deep love for the nation of Israel and how much He desired to give her the best. In return, He expected reciprocated love: "I thought you would call me 'Father'" (Jeremiah 3:19). God had high expectations for His people, but the people did not see the value of His expectations and turned to worthless idols.

In a marriage relationship, couples experience a similar dilemma when high expectations remain unrealized and the relationship begins to feel one-sided.

13. What expectations have you had for your marriage and/or spouse that have not been fulfilled?

How might you adjust your expectations to fit reality?

14. What expectations might your spouse hold that you have not been able to fulfill?

Unmet Needs

Another root conflict in many marriages is unmet needs. The people of Israel sought out other gods to fulfill unmet desires in their hearts. In the end, the people realized that idolatry—looking to things other than God to fulfill their needs—was mere "deception" (Jeremiah 3:23).

15. In what ways did God provide for Israel?

     In your opinion, why did Israel turn away from following God when He fulfilled their needs?

16. What are some of the basic needs that spouses should be meeting for one another?

     What needs might be met by other relationships and activities without threatening the special relationship of a married couple?

Although within the marriage relationship many human needs can and should be met, no one human being can fulfill every need for another; and it is unreasonable to place this expectation on your spouse. This is why God has provided other relationships in our lives. For example, let's say you enjoy taking classes in computer programming, but your spouse has absolutely no interest in computers—not even playing games on them! In contrast, you can't seem to stay awake through one more Book-of-the-Month-Club meeting, and your spouse loves to discuss books and ideas. Should you begin to think that you and your spouse are incompatible because you don't share all of the same interests? Of course not! Instead each of you should encourage the other to pursue his or her interests and enjoy them. One way you can encourage each other is to pray together for God to bring people into each of your lives with whom you can share an interest and also ask Him to bring to mind new interests that you can pursue together as a couple.

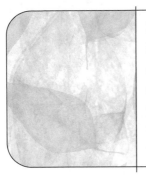

Note: When seeking others who share your same interests, always be mindful to seek others of your same gender. This not only shows respect for your spouse but will demonstrate your dedication to protect your marriage from any opportunity for temptation that might sneak in under the pretense of friendship.

watering the hope

Consider the story of Jason and Ashley.

Jason and Ashley seemed meant for each other from the beginning of their relationship. They spent hours talking, sharing common interests and enjoying one another's company during their courtship, engagement and early months of their marriage. But then they began fighting over seemingly mundane things, such as who should take out the trash, how the table should be set, who should take the car to be serviced and how much money they should spend, save or invest. These little spats soon escalated into more serious quarrels.

Jason had been raised by his mother—a fiercely independent woman who had made a good life for her son and herself in spite of his father leaving her shortly after Jason was born. She had learned to take care of everything they needed to keep them afloat—from housework to investments, from child care to auto repairs—without much outside help. She had a successful career as a realtor, providing well for her son and raising him to be the responsible and loving man he had become. Jason had a great job in sales. He worked long hours in hopes of one day having his own business.

Ashley was the youngest of three siblings and was raised in a traditional family setting. Her parents were great role models of what a marriage should be—they were each others' best friend, sharing everything. Their roles were well defined; her dad took care of everything outside the house and her mom took care of everything inside the house. For the most part her mother had stayed home to raise the children, pursuing a full-time career only after Ashley went off to college. Although Ashley enjoyed her teaching career, she also enjoyed the close family life that she had experienced growing up and hoped to be a stay-at-home mom once she and Jason had children.

Jason felt smothered by Ashley's desire for constant companionship and always wanting to talk and do things together; Ashley was threatened by Jason's need to be alone at times or to do things with his friends. Jason's long hours at work meant Ashley spent time alone at home not always knowing when he would be home for dinner. She longed for the leisurely family dinners that she had enjoyed as a child; Jason preferred to eat quickly and get up and do something productive. Jason wanted Ashley to be more independent and take care of things without his involvement. Ashley wanted Jason to be more attentive and communicative. Their life together seemed to be deteriorating into endless quarrels and sulking silences.[1]

17. What might be the expectations and unmet needs for Jason?

For Ashley?

18. If Jason were your friend, what would be your advice to him?

19. If Ashley were your friend, what would be your advice to her?

20. How might couples avoid the pitfalls of unrealized expectations and unmet needs?

 harvesting the fruit

God does not want our roots of conflict to get in the way of our relationship with Him or each other; but from time to time, the roots will threaten to take hold once again—and when they do, it is okay to become passionate about them. Our desire to stay focused on each other and recognizing, admitting and learning how to handle conflict should be the driving force behind our passion. We are to go to the Lord at all times but even more so while in conflict.

Meditate on 1 Peter 3:11, "He must seek peace and pursue it." In other words, when times get tough—and they will—seek out the Lord and the peace that surpasses all understanding (see Philippians 4:7).

21. When you seek the Lord, what two things will Christ guard in your life (see Philippians 4:7)?

22. Describe one example of how you have seen Christ bring to your attention a root of conflict that had begun to cause tension between you and your spouse.

How did relying on God's peace help you through the situation?

If you have not yet received peace about the situation, what next step will you take in order to assure that the peace of God will soon quiet your heart and your mind on the matter?

Root conflicts can take on many different forms in a marriage relationship. It is quite possible that your root conflicts are anchored in the unrealistic expectations you place on your spouse or what you consider to be your unmet needs.

During the coming week, take the time to begin evaluating your expectations of your spouse. Create a two-column table with the following headings: "Expectation" and "Reasonable/Unreasonable." List your expectations on one side and prayerfully consider for each one whether or not it is reasonable to expect your spouse to fulfill that need.

As you prayerfully do this, you will no doubt find that your spouse cannot fill every expectation you have, and you can begin to resolve any unwarranted resentment that may have been building up since you first realized your spouse isn't everything you expected him or her to be!

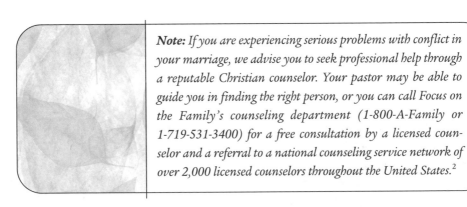

Note: If you are experiencing serious problems with conflict in your marriage, we advise you to seek professional help through a reputable Christian counselor. Your pastor may be able to guide you in finding the right person, or you can call Focus on the Family's counseling department (1-800-A-Family or 1-719-531-3400) for a free consultation by a licensed counselor and a referral to a national counseling service network of over 2,000 licensed counselors throughout the United States.[2]

Notes

1. This is a compilation of several stories. Any resemblance to an actual situation is purely coincidental.
2. Counselors at Focus on the Family are licensed only in the state of Colorado.

how to have a good fight

In your anger do not sin: Do not let the sun go down while you are still angry.
Ephesians 4:26

Recognizing the roots of conflict is the first step in the process of learning how to deal with conflict in your marriage. Once recognition has taken place, it's time to admit to the problem. One dictionary definition of the word "admit" is "to concede as valid; acknowledge to be true."[1] Admitting to a need or fault allows the healing process to continue, as it opens the door to confronting, discussing and, finally, resolving the issue. Most of the time, this process involves two people who care deeply for each other. The passion in a marriage relationship inevitably seeps into how a couple deals with conflict. Why? Because like God, we fight passionately for those things we care most about.

Before a couple can learn how to fight, each partner must know what is worth fighting for. Once you've identified those issues worth fighting for, you'll need to learn when, where and how to fight for them.

tilling the ground

While one couple's fighting habits mirror a yelling match, another couple might emit a cold dose of the silent treatment. However it is that you and your spouse handle conflict, God wants to have you take a step back. He desires conflict to be addressed, yet He wants our passion to be under His control. He wants us to appropriately confront our roots of conflict in order that we might better serve one another with a selfless spirit.

1. When you were growing up, how did your family members typically handle conflict?

2. How do you typically handle conflict?

3. What makes you passionately angry or frustrated in your marriage?

4. Is there a particular time of day when you are more likely to argue with your spouse?

Is there a particular situation or place?

5. What is the silliest thing that you and your spouse have ever argued about?

No matter how similar your and your spouse's backgrounds, expectations, desires and needs, there will always be conflict when two people try to become one. Let's see how to fight the good fight!

---

planting the seed

God is a fighter. Ever since the Fall, when Adam and Eve disobeyed God and spurred on the sin of mankind, God has continually fought for our souls when we seek after Him (see Job 33:23-30).

Examples of God fighting for His people are found throughout Scripture. But why does God fight for a people that has continually turned away from Him? Even more interestingly, what issues are so important to God that He is willing to fight for them?

What Is Worth Fighting For?

At various times in our lives, we will all face extraordinary circumstances requiring extraordinary obedience. Obedience is required in a marriage when the going gets tough. The covenant that unites two individuals into one requires more than an occasional pat on the back or kiss on the forehead; it requires commitment, love and compassion, and faithfulness.

Commitment

In Hosea 2:19, God tells the nation of Israel, "I will betroth you to me forever." He was declaring the ultimate commitment—one that there was no walking away from.

6. How has your spouse demonstrated commitment to you?

   In what ways do you express commitment to your spouse?

Love and Compassion

Hosea 2:19 says, "I will betroth you . . . in love and compassion." The word "love" is so overused in today's culture that its true meaning has virtually been forgotten. We might say that we love our spouse and then say that we love pizza.

What is love? We have many examples of God's love throughout Scripture.

7. What do the following verses say about God's love and compassion for us?

   John 3:16

   John 8:3-11

Romans 5:8

1 John 1:9

8. What are the attributes of godly love described in 1 Corinthians 13:4-8a?

9. What type of love does the Lord describe in Hosea 3:1?

God asked Hosea to show love in an extreme situation as a living example of His own love for His beloved—His people. His purpose was to draw His adulterous betrothed back to Him.

10. What comes to mind when you think of the phrase "unconditional love"?

Is there such a thing as unhealthy unconditional love? How might a relationship be hurt if there were no conditions placed on either spouse?

God loves us as we are, but He does place conditions on His love—He loves us no matter what, but our relationship with Him suffers when we do not reciprocate His love. Despite the circumstances, God *always* loves and *always* welcomes us with open arms when we come to Him. In our relationships, healthy unconditional love says, "I love you as you are. I know I'm not perfect, and I don't expect you to be either. I care about you and I want the best for you. There will be times when I hurt you, but when I do, I promise to do my best to change that part of me." This love is shown through a covenant relationship that sustains itself through your spouse's and your good and bad days.

Faithfulness

Another attribute God mentions in Hosea 2:20 is faithfulness. "I will betroth you in faithfulness, and you will acknowledge the LORD." Committed to His betrothed and unconditional in His love, the Lord also serves as the prime example of how to be faithful and devoted to our spouses.

Despite the wayward and adulterous ways of the people of Israel, God remained faithful to His covenant with Abraham.

11. How has God demonstrated His willingness to fight to maintain His relationship with His beloved?

12. Why is being steadfast and faithful important in a marriage relationship?

13. What outside forces threaten to destroy faithfulness in marriage?

Which ones particularly threaten your own marriage?

Once the nation of Israel recognized and admitted to the conflict (see Jeremiah 3:23-25), God was able to confront the issues that caused the conflict. Acknowledging a problem may take time and courage, but once you've done this, you're on the road to confronting the issues behind the problem— and you've begun to fight for your marriage.

14. What are the big-ticket items worth fighting for in marriage (e.g., fidelity, honesty, etc.)?

15. What seemingly less important issues might be worth fighting for in your marriage (e.g., who is responsible for what duties, where or how to spend the holidays, etc.)?

Once you've discovered the sources of conflict and the things worth fighting for in your marriage, you need to discover how to fight for your marriage.

How Do I Fight for the Things Worth Fighting For?

You may be thinking, *Now that I know something about the causes of conflict, how exactly do I go about resolving conflict?* Let's focus on three areas of discernment and explore when, where and how to handle conflict.

Learn to Discern When

The apostle Paul told us in 1 Corinthians 7:29 that "the time is short." Our earthly days are numbered, and there is no time to waste embittering our lives in anger or in unresolved conflict in our marriages.

"Do not let the sun go down while you are still angry" (Ephesians 4:26). There is more to this verse than meets the eye at first glance. There is sound advice here: Resolving anger before nighttime—when you're fatigued, tired and perhaps on edge from a hard day's work—is ideal. Our Lord Jesus prayed and brought His issues to God during the early morning hours (see Mark 1:35).

16. What particular time of the day are you and your spouse more likely to confront issues?

    What is the usual outcome? Is this the optimum time for both of you to discuss difficult issues or do you end up arguing and not resolving issues?

17. What would be a good time for discussing potential trouble spots in your relationship? When are you both more able to deal with problems?

    Discovering a good time to discuss difficult topics will take some work, but making the effort will be worth it in building and strengthening your marriage.

Learn to Discern Where

Just as Jesus prayed in the early morning hours, He also prayed in "a solitary place" (Mark 1:35). It is effective for a couple to mirror what Jesus did in prayer when they are dealing with conflict. Why? Because when Jesus prayed, He would often bring His difficulties to God in a quiet, reflective and peaceful place where He could feel comfortable releasing His emotions (see Luke 5:16). For this same reason, it is important for a couple that is dealing with difficult issues to choose a quiet, secure, private place when dealing with conflict.

18. Where would be a good place to set aside for resolving conflict with your spouse?

It is probably better to confront each other in the privacy of your own home, perhaps when the children are out and the TV is off, rather than in the grocery store parking lot or at your in-laws' house. In a nutshell, conflict resolution should occur at a time and place that give you and your spouse the best opportunity to work out the issues at hand—without interference or inhibiting factors.

Learn to Discern How

Equally important in resolving conflict is how we react to it. We need to acknowledge our need for God's wisdom and help (see Proverbs 3:5-6) and overcome conflict through action (see Ephesians 4:26), proactively asking God's help in resolving conflict rather than allowing issues to embitter our hearts.

Because God desires for us to resolve conflict and Satan does not, it is important to remember to "not give the devil a foothold" (Ephesians 4:27) by allowing our anger to fester and then explode.

19. How do you deal with conflict in your marriage relationship?

20. What particular situation or issue in your marriage might "give the devil a foothold" in your relationship?

21. What issues have you successfully resolved in your marriage?

22. About what issues might you continue to harbor bitterness and anger?

God commands us to "get rid of all bitterness, rage and anger, brawling and slander, along with every form of malice. Be kind and compassionate to one another, forgiving each other, just as in Christ God forgave you" (Ephesians 4:31-32). We can only do this through His Holy Spirit living and working in us.

Consider the story of Brad and Sharon.

> After only five years of marriage, Brad and Sharon seemed to be at an impasse. Although they had never had a disagreement during their entire courtship, engagement and first year of marriage, it now seemed they disagreed over everything: from who should take out the trash to what car to buy, from where to go for dinner to where to go on vacation and how much to spend. It had gotten so bad that they seldom communicated with one another except to transfer information such as "Dinner's ready" or "Your dad's on the phone."
>
> After an argument that escalated from a disagreement over what side of the plate the fork should be set to a screaming, silverware-dumping diatribe on the fact that he was too demanding and she was a terrible housekeeper, Brad stomped out of the house with a window-rattling slam of the door. He went on a long walk, thinking hard on the state of their marriage and wondering if he should call it quits. As he prayed and walked, it occurred to him that he had a choice: simply walk away from the marriage or fight to save it. He decided he loved their baby—and he'd have to admit that he still loved Sharon—too much to give up. He wanted to fight to save their marriage, but where and how to begin seemed beyond him.[2]

23. Aside from the obvious idea of seeking counseling, what do you think should be Brad's first steps in resolving their differences?

24. What are some possible reasons that Sharon and Brad's conflicts were increasing?

25. In the early stages of their relationship, the fact that they never disagreed was probably a symptom of problems to come. What might have been happening during these early years that later led to their present difficulties?

26. What might be some rules to fighting the good fight when conflicts do arise?

 harvesting the fruit

Despite the difficulties we face in our lives and in our marriages, God wants us to return to each other, just as He told Israel to return to Him (see Jeremiah 3:14; 4:1). Remember, it is God's desire for your marriage to be a place for maturation and growth, both in your relationship as a couple and with Him.

God Himself provided us with a picture of how we can achieve a fulfilling marriage. He didn't give up when the quick fix wasn't working—in fact, He spent hundreds of years fighting for Israel's love, endlessly reaching out to His people only to be pushed away. When the people of Israel finally returned to their love-stricken Lord, He accepted them with open arms.

God desires and has shown us that this patient and enduring attitude will win in the end. It is only through such a poignant message that couples will learn what it truly means to never give up, to persevere and to fight for the good of their marriage.

27. What are your usual reactions when conflict occurs?

28. Do you expect fast results when resolving conflict or do you give up easily?

29. Are you willing to persevere in your marriage, acknowledging and resolving conflict when it arises instead of giving up and walking away?

God knows that we are imperfect—He was there when it happened! Still, He wants us to reach for the best He has for us in our marriages.

Make a decision to live more passionately today. Choose one area in your marriage that you feel needs an extra push. Perhaps it is communication or maybe it is self-control. No matter what the area, commit to persevering through it until you and your spouse can recognize a significant improvement. Track your progress weekly on a calendar or in a personal journal, and just watch what God will do with your efforts!

Notes
1. *Merriam-Webster's Collegiate Dictionary*, 10th ed., s.v. "admit."
2. This is a compilation of several stories. Any resemblance to an actual situation is purely coincidental.

keep talking

Do not let any unwholesome talk come out of your mouths, but only what is helpful
for building others up according to their needs, that it may benefit those who listen.
Ephesians 4:29

Communication is vital to any healthy relationship. Unfortunately, there are
some who feel that the less something is talked about, the better the situation will be. This is especially dangerous in a marriage relationship.

As is often the case in many marriages, spouses come into a marriage with
varying degrees of communication skills and styles. It takes a great deal of
effort and perseverance to learn to communicate well—and even the best
communicators do not always succeed. The key is to keep working at it.

tilling the ground

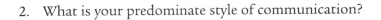

One of the most important elements for healthy communication within a marriage is patience. Why? Because as shown by God in His dealings with Israel, patience is the key that opens the door to two-sided talk.

1. What do you consider important elements of healthy communication?

2. What is your predominate style of communication?

    How does your spouse's communication style differ from yours?

3. What are some other forms of communication besides verbal?

Whether you and your spouse are Chatty Cathy and Chatty Charlie or Silent Sally and Silent Sam—or somewhere in between—you need to learn to communicate with your spouse in ways that will help your relationship mature.

God is the ultimate communicator. Throughout the Bible, He has given us many models of different ways to communicate.

Speak Tenderly

When Israel betrayed God by following worthless idols, His anger and wrath poured forth (see Jeremiah 1:16). However, when He instructed Jeremiah on what to say to the people, He also spoke tender words: "Return, faithless Israel . . . I will frown on you no longer, for I am merciful, . . . I will not be angry forever" (Jeremiah 3:12).

It is amazing to think that God's love for His people did not fail in spite of their betrayal. What is the first thing we feel when we are betrayed? It's definitely *not* love, is it? When we are angry or frustrated, we find it hard (if not impossible) to feel love and to speak with a gentle spirit.

4. How does God begin His indictment of Israel in Jeremiah 2:2-3?

How can God's technique of using tender memories help us communicate with our spouse?

5. It is easy to react negatively when we are hurt, frustrated or angry. What are some practical actions that can help you speak tenderly to your spouse (and others) when you are hurt, frustrated or angry?

There is a saying that goes something like this: "Let your words to others be tender—you may have to eat them!" God's Word states it this way: "Pleasant words are a honeycomb, sweet to the soul and healing to the bones" (Proverbs 16:24).

Speak Openly

A healthy relationship requires open communication. A person who can freely vent to his or her spouse without the fear of being rebuked will communicate more often and more openly.

The psalmists freely expressed their frustrations to the Lord (see Psalms 22:1-2; 94:1-3). They had confidence that what they shared would be thoughtfully and lovingly considered by God.

6. Why is it a fearful thing to express deeply felt emotions to someone you love?

7. How can you demonstrate your willingness to listen to your spouse when he or she needs to express deeply felt emotions such as anger, fear, frustration, etc.?

There will be times when you or your spouse will need to vent difficult feelings. When you thoughtfully and lovingly consider what's being said, you are showing God's love toward your spouse. If you truly desire to have open communication in your marriage, you must be willing to allow your spouse to be vulnerable with his or her feelings without fear of being rejected or ignored.

Speak Honestly

Communicating honestly requires that we neither sugarcoat issues nor avoid uncomfortable or difficult subjects. It also requires that we admit mistakes and accept criticism graciously.

Although God began His confrontation of Israel's sin tenderly (see Jeremiah 2:2-3), He honestly stated His case against them in Jeremiah 2:4–3:5.

8. How does Jeremiah 3:4-5 point out Israel's dishonesty about her behavior?

9. Why is it difficult to deal with uncomfortable issues or to admit mistakes to our spouse?

We live in a culture that no longer honors honesty. When politicians, corporate executives and even clergy are caught in their lies, they try to explain their way out of their behavior or they blame others for their predicament. Some might even reason that it is better to tell a little white lie rather than hurt someone's feelings. Others might alter the truth to avoid accepting the consequences of their behavior.

10. What might be some motivations of someone who is not being honest?

11. What does Colossians 3:9-10 say about dishonesty?

How does dishonesty damage a marriage relationship?

12. Why do you think the Lord instructs us to speak the truth to one another?

God explicitly tells us how we are to communicate with others: "Do not let any unwholesome talk come out of your mouths, but only what is helpful for building others up according to their needs, that it may benefit those who listen" (Ephesians 4:29).

13. How can the command in Ephesians 4:29 be applied to being honest in our marriage relationship?

Speak Boldly

In Ezekiel 2:6-7, God instructed Ezekiel to speak to Israel and not to be afraid of the response he might receive to what God told him to say.

Like Ezekiel, we will encounter times when we must speak words of truth to someone who does not want to hear them. It is very difficult to be vulnerable with someone who might react negatively, but there's a reason for boldness—to proclaim the truth.

In speaking boldly to your spouse, your focus should be on speaking the truth so that the result is that the two of you will deal with a difficult issue and grow in your relationship.

14. Have you ever had an experience in which you had to speak boldly to someone about something they were doing that hurt your relationship with them? Or has someone had to speak boldly to you about your own behavior? What was the result?

15. How do you know when you should speak to someone about something that is hurting your relationship?

We need to develop the ability to speak boldly. Whether it is something as simple as asking your spouse for help with household chores or something as serious as confronting sinful behavior, speaking out when necessary will help our relationship grow.

Listen Carefully

One aspect of communication that is often neglected is the art of listening. We need to learn to listen attentively as we communicate with others.

16. Have you ever been in conversation with another person and realized that he or she was not listening to you? How did you know you were not being listened to?

What communicates to you that a person is truly listening to you?

We are often so busy thinking of the next thing we want to say that we do not really hear what the other person is saying. Listening involves caring for the other person and being empathetic to him or her. A good listener tries to understand the feelings behind the words.

17. What does James 1:19 say about the art of listening?

How can this admonition be put into practice in a marriage?

Listening requires understanding the other person's state of mind as well as their words. It will require totally focusing on him or her and not on your own feelings or thoughts; this means that you will need to stop anything else that you might be doing—watching TV, fixing dinner, etc.—sit down, give him or her your full attention and look him or her in the eye. You will also need to show acceptance of the other person—even if you disagree with what is being said—allowing him or her the opportunity to speak.

At times the person may not be able to express him- or herself well—especially when emotionally upset—so you will need to read between the lines, ask pertinent questions and repeat back what you think you are hearing. Good listening requires you to be a student of the other person's communication style.

watering the hope

Much literature has been written regarding communication styles, with topics ranging from the difference between how men and women communicate to how couples speak different love languages. While we will hit on a few key differences in communication styles, it is important to note that we will be skimming the surface of a very deep subject. If you need more help in this area, we encourage you to refer to some other resources.[1]

Communication styles are dependent on many different factors including gender, learning style, personality type, family influences and past experiences. Two main sources of difficulty between different communication styles are the amount of words used and the volume of our conversations.

Amount

The amount of words one speaks can vary greatly between husbands and wives. One spouse may use a lot of words to say something while the other uses the fewest words possible (or doesn't say anything at all!). Because spouses are meant to be a complement to one another, their personalities are usually quite different. One spouse might be an introvert who needs times of quiet and only converses when necessary while the other might be an extrovert who requires constant activity and wants to talk about everything. Consider the story of Mike and Jill.

Mike and Jill are a happy, compatible couple. They enjoy doing many of the same things, but Jill has begun to notice that she does most of the talking, and Mike just sits and listens, rarely responding with any questions or input. When Mike does speak, he uses as few words as possible, which Jill finds frustrating because she often finds herself misunderstanding his intent.

What's the matter with Mike? Jill thinks to herself. *Why doesn't he talk to me? Is he hiding something? Why doesn't he ever want to share how he's feeling?* Jill is interpreting Mike's quietness as disinterest, while Mike is content to listen to Jill and doesn't feel the need to respond or share his feelings unless he feels strongly one way or the other about the subject at hand. Mike has no clue that his silence is hurting Jill, and Jill has no clue as to why Mike rarely seems to have anything to say![2]

18. Brainstorm some ways that Mike and Jill can work to achieve a healthier balance in their communication styles.

19. How do you and your spouse differ in the amount of words you use to communicate?

What have you done to compensate for your differences?

Volume

The volume of our conversations is usually influenced by our personality type and by our family experiences. Some people speak loudly or with great emotion. Others might speak quietly or with a reserved tone.

As the youngest child growing up, Becky never felt heard. With older brothers and two busy parents, she immediately learned that if she were to be heard, she must raise her voice and speak over the voices and activities of everyone and everything around her.

John grew up an only child in a single-parent home where he never raised his voice. He and his mother had a very quiet household and spoke in soft, reserved tones. John's father on the other hand was loud and boisterous, especially when he was angry. During John's occasional visits with his father, he would withdraw whenever his father became loud and boisterous, causing a strain in their relationship that is still unresolved.

In their marriage, the differing communication styles of Becky and John proved difficult. Becky interpreted John's soft, reserved style to mean that he didn't care about the topic at hand, while John felt that Becky never really listened to him because she was always interrupting him. He also felt threatened when she became loud or emotional and would withdraw from the conversation.[3]

20. How can two people with different styles and personalities learn to communicate?

21. What aspects of your upbringing and personality do you see contributing to how you currently communicate?

How does that differ from your spouse's background and personality?

It's important to remember that fighting for your marriage includes fighting to improve the communication between you and your spouse. Take a proactive stand and ask God to reveal any differences between your communication styles, and once you recognize those differences, work together to make them compatible.

 harvesting the fruit

Effective communication is a two-way street. If you are having difficulty walking on the same side of that street with your spouse, make a concerted effort this week to pray for a reconciliation of the differences between your styles.

22. How has your spouse demonstrated the following?

Speaking tenderly

Speaking honestly

Speaking boldly

Listening carefully

23. Which of these areas do you personally need to work to improve?

What will you do this week to begin to demonstrate those aspects of communication?

24. List the ways that you and your spouse differ in communication style and how they have affected your relationship.

List at least three action steps you will take to improve your communication.

After sharing your answers with your spouse, pray together. Thank God for each other and for your different styles and personalities. Express to Him what you appreciate about your spouse. Ask Him to help the two of you to hone your communication skills. Commit to at least one of the action steps that you wrote down.

Make a date to get away from your daily responsibilities and just talk!

Notes

1. Some resources to help you understand your communication and personality styles include H. Norman Wright, *Communication: Key to Your Marriage* (Ventura, CA: Regal Books, 2000); and Gary Chapman, *The Five Love Languages* (Chicago: Northfield Publishing, 1992).
2. This is a compilation of several stories. Any resemblance to an actual situation is purely coincidental.
3. This is a compilation of several stories. Any resemblance to an actual situation is purely coincidental.

caring enough to confront

God disciplines us for our good, that we may share in his holiness.
No discipline seems pleasant at the time, but painful. Later on, however,
it produces a harvest of righteousness and peace.
Hebrews 12:10-11

The following scenario is all-too common in so many homes:

"But that's the fourth night this week," Charla said as the tears sprung into her eyes. "I know this project is important, but . . . but . . ." As the tears began to fall and her voice thickened with emotion, she managed to squeak out a good-bye and hang up the phone before she broke down completely. She retreated to her bedroom, so the children couldn't see her crying. She was exhausted from taking care of everything at home while Wes worked night and day at his company. Once again she began to wonder why Wes seemed to be spending less and less time with her and the children. He was even missing church. If he wasn't working on Sundays, he was too tired to go with them when he was home. Her thoughts raced ahead. *Is he having an affair? Maybe he doesn't love me any more. What would happen if he left me with three small children to raise?* She tried to keep the house in order and herself in good shape and not burden him with her concerns. The angry voices of her two older children, Amy and Joey, interrupted her thoughts and then the baby, Mandy, began to howl. Charla quickly washed her own tearful face. As she ran to the kitchen to see what was wrong, she realized that something needed to happen or their marriage was headed on a collision course with disaster.[1]

Most couples begin married life with the expectation of enjoying life, supporting one another, raising children and growing old—together. Somehow in the hustle and bustle of modern life, the dream gets skewed by too many demands on their time and energy or by temptations to stray. When one spouse begins to drift in a marriage, the other spouse needs to confront the situation before they drift too far and there's little hope of rescue.

How will you deal with areas of difficulty in your marriage? Will you ignore them and let them fester into bitterness or isolation between you and your spouse? Or will you care enough to confront the problem and stop it dead in its tracks?

1. What difficult situations or wrong behaviors or actions should be confronted in any relationship—whether with a spouse, relative or friend?

    Are there behaviors or actions that shouldn't (or needn't) be confronted? Explain.

2. Have you ever had to confront someone about something they were doing that was wrong or hurtful? What was the result?

3. Has someone ever confronted you about something you were doing wrong? How did you react?

    What was the result?

Whether we must confront someone because he or she said something that hurt our feelings or because he or she is being blatantly sinful, we can look to God's example of why, when, how and where to confront another's behavior.

planting the seed

God dealt with Israel's rebellion by showing tough love, speaking passionate words, persevering and then extending grace to them in order to reconcile His people to Himself.

Tough Love

God confronts His beloved because He loves them (see Hebrews 12:5-6). And while discipline or confrontation might not be pleasant at the time—and might, indeed be rather painful—God confronts destructive behavior because He knows that discipline will eventually produce "a harvest of righteousness and peace" (Hebrews 12:11).

4. How does Hebrews 12:12-15 relate to confronting someone about his or her behavior?

When we refuse to obey God, He will discipline us to produce "a harvest of righteousness and peace." There are examples throughout the Bible of how He disciplined those He loved. He exerts tough love to help us mature and grow in our relationship with Him.

Tough love means dealing with a problem or situation by doing and/or saying something that is hard. It might mean asking for a time of separation until the offending party makes a choice to change his or her hurtful behavior.

Tough love insists that until changes are made, the status quo of the relationship cannot continue.[2]

5. Has there been a time when you felt God's discipline—His tough love? What was your experience and the result?

Passionate Words

When your spouse does not respond to words of kindness, it is time to take your love one step further. Just as God did, you need to verbalize the problem and what needs to be done.

6. According to Ezekiel 16:35-43, what did the nation of Israel do to anger God?

7. According to Hosea 2:9-13, to what extremes did God go to get Israel to respond to His tough love?

8. How do you think passionate communication would better help a couple resolve a marital conflict?

9. Why is it important for both spouses to show an interest in and a concern for confronting problems in their relationship?

How would you feel if your spouse told you that he or she couldn't care less if the two of you worked out a problem?

There may come a time when you will have to give your spouse an ultimatum: he or she must change a behavior or attitude to avoid the consequences of further hurt or estrangement.

Perseverance

After Israel turned from God to worship idols, God continued pursuing Israel. He loved them beyond measure and never gave up His pursuit. The point is clear: God wanted His beloved back and was ready to say and do whatever was necessary to draw her back to Him.

10. In Jeremiah 3:12-14, how did God react to Israel's disobedient actions?

11. What characteristics did God display as He drew Israel back to Him?

12. How can we fight for what we love?

13. How can we apply this attitude of perseverance in our marriage?

God so loved Israel that He was willing to confront her rebelliousness, persevering until she repented and returned to Him.

Grace

God extended grace to Israel many times. His forgiveness was always available to His people when they repented, but it was up to them to ask for and accept God's favor.

14. Read Ezekiel 16:59-63. What was God's accusation against His people?

How did He demonstrate grace toward them?

15. What did God establish to make atonement for their sin?

16. Why do you think God continued to confront and fight for His people's love?

17. How would a commitment to extend grace and forgiveness bolster a marriage relationship?

18. Why is it difficult for a married couple to extend and accept forgiveness from each other?

Reconciliation

The results of God's tough love, passionate words, perseverance and grace led to reconciliation between Him and Israel. God passionately declared in Jeremiah 3:12, "Return, faithless Israel . . . I will frown on you no longer."

The Lord's desire for His people was to become one with Him, like a wife to her husband.

19. How does Hosea 2:16 express God's desire for reconciliation?

20. How does reconciliation foster a deeper and more personal relationship with your spouse?

God gave His beloved many opportunities to repent and turn from her rebelliousness. He exercised tough love, passionate words, perseverance and grace to bring them back to Him. Think about this: If God hadn't provided Israel with a second chance by exercising tough love but had instead thrown in the towel after Israel's first rebellious act, would there have been a reconciliation?

An Example of Biblical Confrontation

You might ask, "But how do I confront someone in a way that achieves positive results?" The biblical account of the prophet Nathan's confrontation of King David concerning his sinful behavior with Bathsheba and Uriah is an example of a successful encounter.[3] Read the story in 2 Samuel 12:1-14.

21. What effective technique did Nathan use to confront David?

22. Why do you think the use of a word picture (story) worked so effectively?

23. How could this technique be useful in a situation in which you need to be confrontational?

24. What might be some other things to do in preparation for a confrontation?

watering the hope

Consider the story of Matt and Heather.

> After nearly two years of marriage, Matt and Heather were beginning to notice that their life together wasn't a fairy tale anymore. Stresses from their jobs, family and finances were seemingly taking a toll on the newlyweds. Heather would return home from work, change clothes and then immediately go to the gym or her parents' home. She'd usually return just as Matt was ready to go to bed and she was too tired to talk at length. Matt felt rejected by Heather's extended absences from home. When they did have a free evening, she always wanted to spend it with their friends or see a movie; there seemed to be no time alone with her anymore.
>
> Matt spent much time in fervent prayer, asking for God's guidance. He eventually came to the realization that he needed to act as soon as possible. His love for Heather was too deep to let her actions continue, just as his hurt was growing deeper too. He wasn't willing to give up and call it quits, but he knew he needed God's help to see this through to the end.
>
> For several days, Matt rehearsed what he would say to Heather. He made plans for a very romantic dinner and a walk on the beach afterwards during which he would state his case.[4]

25. Outline a word picture (story) that Matt could use to confront the problem in his marriage.

26. What further suggestions might you give Matt?

27. What would you do if you were involved in such a situation? How would you resolve, or mend, the disconnection in your marriage?

harvesting the fruit

If you are dealing with a rebellious spouse or difficult circumstance, today could be the first day toward your reconciled relationship. Try to focus on the end result instead of today's stresses. "Do not worry about tomorrow, for tomorrow will worry about itself" (Matthew 6:34).

28. Write down 10 positive things that you appreciate about your spouse.

Share the 10 things you listed with your spouse.

29. What is something that concerns you about your relationship with your spouse? Think of a word picture (story) that would express your concerns. Share your concerns in an attitude of love.

Read John 13:1-17 together. "Now that you know these things, you will be blessed if you do them" (v. 17). Wash one another's feet. When you are done, pray together, thanking God for the opportunity to love and serve your spouse. Ask for His healing grace to cover your relationship.

Notes

1. This is a compilation of several stories. Any resemblance to an actual situation is purely coincidental.
2. For more information on confronting a situation requiring tough love, refer to Dr. James Dobson, *Love Must Be Tough* (Waco, TX: Word Books, 1983).
3. For more information on how to use the word-picture technique described, refer to Gary Smalley and John Trent, *The Language of Love* (Waco, TX: Word Books, 1988).
4. This is a compilation of several stories. Any resemblance to an actual situation is purely coincidental.

leader's discussion guide

General Guidelines

1. If at all possible, the group should be led by a married couple. This does not mean that both spouses need to be leading the discussions; perhaps one spouse is better at facilitating discussions while the other is better at relationship building or organization—but the leader couple should share responsibilities wherever possible.

2. At the first meeting, be sure to lay down the ground rules for discussions, stressing that following these rules will help everyone feel comfortable during discussion times.

   a. No one should share anything of a personal or potentially embarrassing nature without first asking his or her spouse's permission.

   b. Whatever is discussed in the group meetings is to be held in strictest confidence among group members only.

   c. Allow everyone in the group to participate. However, as a leader, don't force anyone to answer a question if he or she is reluctant. Be sensitive to the different personalities and communication styles among your group members.

3. Fellowship time is very important in building small-group relationships. Providing beverages and/or light refreshments either before or after each session will encourage a time of informal fellowship.

4. Most people live very busy lives; respect the time of your group members by beginning and ending meetings on time.

The Focus on the Family Marriage Ministry Guide *has even more information on starting and leading a small group. You will find this an invaluable resource as you lead others through this Bible study.*

How to Use the Material

1. Each session has more than enough material to cover in a 45-minute teaching period. You will probably not have time to discuss every single question in each session, so prepare for each meeting by selecting questions you feel are most important to address for your group; discuss other questions as time permits. Be sure to save the last 10 minutes of your meeting time for each couple to interact individually and to pray together before adjourning.

    Optional Eight-Session Plan—You can easily divide each session into two parts if you'd like to cover all of the material presented in each session. Each section of the session has enough questions to divide in half, and the Bible study sections (Planting the Seed) are divided into two or three sections that can be taught in separate sessions.

2. Each spouse should have his or her own copy of the book in order to personally answer the questions. The general plan of this study is that the couples complete the questions at home during the week and then bring their books to the meeting to share what they have learned during the week.

    However, the reality of leading small groups in this day and age is that some members will find it difficult to do the homework. If you find that to be the case with your group, consider adjusting the lessons and having members complete the study during your meeting time as you guide them through the lesson. If you use this method, be sure to encourage members to share their individual answers with their spouses during the week (perhaps on a date night).

Session One | The Causes of Conflict

A Note to Leaders: This Bible study series is based on The Marriage Masterpiece[1] *by Al Janssen. We highly recommend that you read chapters 10 and 11 in preparation for leading this study.*

Before the Meeting

1. Gather materials for making name tags in addition to extra pens, paper, 3x5-inch index cards and Bibles.
2. Make photocopies of the Prayer Request Form (see *The Focus on the Family Marriage Ministry Guide,* "Reproducible Forms" section) or provide index cards for recording requests.
3. Read through your own answers from the session and mark the ones that you especially want to have the group discuss. Also highlight any key verses you feel are appropriate to share.
4. Prepare slips of paper with references for the verses that you will want someone to read aloud during the session. Distribute these slips as group members arrive, but be sensitive to those who are uncomfortable reading aloud or who might not be familiar with the Bible.
5. Obtain a newsprint pad or poster board and a felt-tip pen or use a white board or chalkboard.

Ice Breakers

1. If this is the first meeting for this couples group, have everyone introduce themselves and tell the group a brief summary of how they met their spouse, how long they have been married and one interesting fact about their spouse. Be sure to remind them not to reveal anything about their spouse that the spouse would be uncomfortable sharing him- or herself.
2. Invite couples to share a favorite Bible verse or love song that reminds them of their love for each other.

Discussion

1. **Tilling the Ground**—Invite members to share their answers to question 1. Have a volunteer write the listed sources of conflict on the newsprint or board as members share. Then have the group vote on the top five sources of conflict. Since questions 2 and 3 are very personal, explain that their answers should be discussed in private with their spouse.

2. **Planting the Seed**—Discuss questions 4-12 and 15-16, briefly reviewing the commentary as transitions between the questions.

3. **Watering the Hope**—The case study and questions in this section will help members bring the Bible study into the reality of their own expectations versus God's plan. Don't neglect this part of the study, as it brings the whole lesson into the here and now, applying God's Word to daily life.

    Read the story of Jason and Ashley and discuss the questions.

4. **Harvesting the Fruit**—Write the word "conflict" in the center of the newsprint pad (poster board, white board or chalkboard) and draw a circle around it. Invite members to call out the different causes of conflict and write the words around the outside of the circled word. If the group is at first quiet, offer one of your own ideas and write it down on the tablet. Connect each word to the circle with a line. Encourage the members to share their ideas until the page is filled with words connecting to the circled word. Close the activity by sharing that the conflicts they listed should be an encouragement to one another, because they are not the only ones who struggle with conflicts.

    This section is meant to help the individual couples apply the lesson to their own marriage and can be dealt with in several ways.

    a. Allow the couples one-on-one time at the end of the meeting. This would require space for them to be alone, with enough space between couples to allow for quiet, private conversations.

        If couples have already answered the questions individually, now would be the time to share their answers. Give a time limit, emphasizing that their discussions can be continued at home if they are not able to answer all of the questions in the time allotted.

        If couples have not answered the questions before the meeting, have them answer them together now. This works best when there is open-ended time for the couples to stay until they have completed their discussion and will require that the leaders stay until the last couple has finished.

b. Instruct couples to complete this section at home during the week after the meeting. This will give them quiet and private time to deal with any issues that might come up and to spend all the time needed to complete the discussion. You will want to follow up at the next meeting to hold couples accountable for completing this part of the lesson.

c. At times it might be advantageous to pair up two couples to discuss these questions. This would help build accountability into the study.

5. **Close in Prayer**—An important part of any small-group relationship is the time spent in prayer for one another. This may also be done in a number of ways.

a. Have couples write out their specific prayer requests on the Prayer Request Forms (or index cards). These requests may then be shared with the whole group or traded with another couple as prayer partners for the week. If requests are shared with the whole group, pray as a group before adjourning the meeting; if requests are traded, allow time for the prayer-partner couples to pray together.

b. Gather the whole group together and lead couples in guided prayer.

c. Have individual couples pray together.

d. Split the members into two groups by sex. Have the men pray over their marriages and ask that God would reveal any conflict that needs addressing. Have the women pray for the conflict resolution skills that they and their husbands need while addressing conflict.

After the Meeting

1. **Evaluate**—Spend time evaluating the meeting's effectiveness (see *The Focus on the Family Marriage Ministry Guide*, "Reproducible Forms" section).

2. **Encourage**—During the week, try to contact each couple (through phone calls, notes of encouragement, or e-mails or instant messaging) and welcome them to the group. Make yourself available to answer any questions or concerns they may have and generally get to know them. This contact might best be done by the husband-leader contacting the

men and the wife-leader contacting the women.

3. **Equip**—Complete the Bible study, even if you have previously gone through this study together.

4. **Pray**—Prayerfully prepare for the next meeting, praying for each couple and your own preparation. Discuss with the Lord any apprehension, excitement or anything else that is on your mind regarding your Bible study material and/or the group members. If you feel inadequate or unprepared, ask for strength and insight. If you feel tired or burdened, ask for God's light yoke. Whatever it is you need, ask God for it. He will provide!

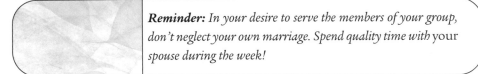

Reminder: In your desire to serve the members of your group, don't neglect your own marriage. Spend quality time with your spouse during the week!

Session Two | How to Have a Good Fight

Before the Meeting

1. Gather materials for making name tags in addition to extra pens, paper, 3x5-inch index cards and Bibles.
2. Make photocopies of the Prayer Request Form or provide index cards for recording requests.
3. Read through your own answers from the session and mark the ones that you especially want to have the group discuss. Also highlight any key verses you feel are appropriate to share.
4. Prepare slips of paper with references for the verses that you will want someone to read aloud during the session. Distribute these slips as group members arrive, but be sensitive to those who are uncomfortable reading aloud or who might not be familiar with the Bible.

Ice Breakers

1. Invite couples to share how they applied to their marriage relationship what they learned in last week's session. Some suggested questions to ask:
   a. What new knowledge did you gain from the discussion you and your spouse had about conflict in your marriage?
   b. What new ideas or actions did you decide on as a result of your discussion?
   c. What changes have you and your spouse made regarding handling conflict in your marriage?
2. Distribute Prayer Request Forms (or index cards) and ask members to write down one praise or good thing that happened last week. Ask volunteers to share their praise. This is a good chance for those who might not always see the good in things to learn how to express gratitude and thanksgiving to God no matter what the circumstance.

Discussion

1. **Tilling the Ground**—Ask volunteers to share their answers to questions 1 and 4, reminding them not to share anything that might embarrass their spouse unless their spouse gives permission. Encourage couples to reflect on their answers to questions 2 and 3 during their Harvesting the Fruit time.

2. **Planting the Seed**—Discuss questions 6-15 in the What's Worth Fighting For? section.

   Read Ephesians 4:26-27 and discuss: What does it mean not to sin in your anger? How can you practice the command not to allow the sun to go down while you are still angry? How does anger give the devil a foothold in a relationship?

   Since the questions in the How Do I Fight for the Things Worth Fighting For? section should primarily be discussed by each couple alone, ask members to share in general on the various topics of this section: Learn to Discern When, Learn to Discern Where and Learn to Discern How.

3. **Watering the Hope**—Read Brad and Sharon's story and discuss question 23. Have each couple pair up with another couple and have the groups of four discuss questions 23-25. Then bring the whole group together and ask for volunteers to share their ideas regarding question 26. Write their suggestions on newsprint, poster board, a white board or chalkboard.

4. **Harvesting the Fruit**—Ask a volunteer to read this section aloud to the group. Invite members to discuss why identifying weaknesses in their marriage will strengthen the relationship. Remind members to track their progress for this exercise in a calendar or journal or in some other way.

5. **Close in Prayer**—This session might have brought some powerful issues to the surface, so accept any personal prayer requests before you close in prayer. If members share specific concerns, be sure to pray for these requests before they leave the meeting. If a sensitive topic is brought out, be sure to talk with the couple afterwards and encourage them.

After the Meeting

1. **Evaluate**—Spend time evaluating the meeting's effectiveness.
2. **Encourage**—Send a note of encouragement to each couple before the next session. Call any couples that may have voiced specific concerns about conflict.
3. **Equip**—Complete next week's Bible study.
4. **Pray**—Pray specifically for each couple. Ask God to guide them through the course of the week and to bring them to next week's session refreshed.

Session Three | Keep Talking

Before the Meeting

1. Gather extra pens, paper, 3x5-inch index cards and Bibles.
2. Make photocopies of the Prayer Request Form or provide index cards for recording requests.
3. Read through your own answers from the session and mark the ones that you especially want to have the group discuss. Also highlight any key verses you feel are appropriate to share.
4. Prepare slips of paper with references for the verses that you will want someone to read aloud during the session. Distribute these slips as group members arrive, but be sensitive to those who are uncomfortable reading aloud or who might not be familiar with the Bible.
5. Prepare a message as described in Ice Breakers option 1. Have it written out so that you can read it to the members. Develop a message that is brief but has particular details such as dates, times, meeting locations, street names and so on.

    If you are doing the option 2 ice breaker, prepare the slips of paper with couples' names.

Ice Breakers

1. Hand Prayer Request Forms (or index cards) to members as they enter the meeting room. Encourage them to complete their prayer requests before the session begins.
2. **Option 1:** Explain that the group will be playing a communication game. The goal is to pass along a message as accurately as possible. Ask for three or four volunteers. Send them out of the room so that they cannot hear your explanation. Ask for one more volunteer to whom you will read the message that you have prepared. Then call in one person from outside and have the volunteer who listened to the message give the message to the person who just came in. Then the second person will tell the message to the third person and continue until all of those who left the room have been told the message. The results could be quite comical.

The point is fairly obvious—communication may be easily misconstrued. Conclude by explaining the importance of communication and how it can be altered depending on our own perceptions, listening abilities, preoccupations and so on.

2. **Option 2:** Write down on slips of paper the names of famous couples—Bible characters, fictional characters, modern celebrities, historical couples, etc.—one couple's name on each slip of paper and play a game of Charades: a couple draws a slip of paper and acts out (without allowing an opportunity for any discussion beforehand) the famous couple, while the other members guess their identity. It will be interesting to see how couples are able to convey messages to one another without verbal communication beforehand. At the conclusion of the game, point out how they were able to communicate with one another without using words.

Discussion

1. **Tilling the Ground**—Discuss questions 1-3.
2. **Planting the Seed**—Briefly review each subheading's commentary and invite members to discuss the questions. This might be a good opportunity to divide the class into smaller discussion groups by gender.
3. **Watering the Hope**—If you did form smaller groups for the Planting the Seed discussion, gather the whole group together to discuss the stories. Remind the members that just as communication can be misconstrued when fed through so many channels—as they witnessed in the game—it can also be misconstrued when two people are speaking in differing styles. Discuss the scenarios.
4. **Harvesting the Fruit**—Invite couples to spend one-on-one time discussing their answers to questions 22-24. Encourage them to decide on one action step they will take this week toward better communication and allow them time to pray together.
5. **Close in Prayer**—Have couples trade prayer request forms (or index cards) with another couple. Direct members to place their prayer-partner's index card as a marker in their Bible, journal or in a place where it will remind them to pray daily. Invite a member or two to close in prayer.

After the Meeting

1. **Evaluate**—Spend time evaluating the meeting's effectiveness.
2. **Encourage**—Ask the prayer partners to contact each other at least once in the coming week for encouragement and support.
3. **Equip**—Complete next week's Bible study and reflect on any key areas that the Holy Spirit speaks to you about during your study.
4. **Pray**—Spend five minutes a day praying for each couple.

Session Four | Caring Enough to Confront

Before the Meeting

1. Provide pens or pencils and Bibles as needed.
2. Make photocopies of the Study Review Form (see *The Focus on the Family Marriage Ministry Guide,* "Reproducible Forms" section).
3. Make photocopies of the Prayer Request Form or provide index cards for recording requests.
4. Read through your own answers from the session and mark the ones that you especially want to have the group discuss. Also highlight any key verses you feel are appropriate to share.
5. Prepare slips of paper with references for the verses that you will want someone to read aloud during the session. Distribute these slips as group members arrive, but be sensitive to those who are uncomfortable reading aloud or who might not be familiar with the Bible.
6. Prepare for one of the Ice Breaker options:
   a. **Option 1:** Collect newspaper and magazine comics that depict people in conflict, whether they are doing so verbally or nonverbally. If you're having difficulty finding appropriate clippings, create sample scenarios of couples interacting and write them on index cards.
   b. **Option 2:** As you call couples during the week, ask them if they have a story they could share with the group that involves a strange or funny confrontation. Ask them to get their spouse's permission if the story involves their spouse or spouse's relatives. Or you could share one of your own (with appropriate permission, of course!).
7. If you are going to have couples do the foot washing at the end of the meeting time, gather the following materials: a towel, a travel-sized bar of soap and a wash basin for each couple; pitchers of warm water; a container to empty the used water into.

Ice Breakers

1. **Option 1:** Display the newspaper comics (or the index cards with scenarios) on the wall or a sheet of poster board and invite individual couples to read them and choose one that they would like to read to the group. Ask them to share why they chose that particular clipping. Share that the prevalence of so many comics depicting conflict shows that this is a common occurrence in relationships.

2. **Option 2:** Invite a volunteer to share about the strangest or funniest conflict he or she has ever had. If it involves his or her spouse, make sure that the volunteer has his or her spouse's permission to share. If it involves someone else, suggest that they not mention the person's name.

Discussion

1. **Tilling the Ground**—Discuss both parts of question 1. Invite volunteers to share their responses to questions 2 and 3.

2. **Planting the Seed**—Discuss questions 4-20, asking volunteers to read the Scripture passages referred to in the questions. Emphasize that despite all of Israel's wayward acts, the Lord still forgave her when she repented. Ask couples to reflect on how they would have acted if they were in God's shoes.

3. **Watering the Hope**—Read the story about Matt and Heather; then have the group members separate into two groups by gender. Instruct the two small groups to discuss questions 25 and 26 and to create a brief word picture (story) that Matt could use to confront Heather's behavior. Give them a few minutes and have each group share their story.

4. **Harvesting the Fruit**—Instruct spouses to share their lists of 10 positive things with their spouse. Then tell them that you have provided equipment and water for them to wash their beloved's feet. If possible, play worship music during this time.

5. **Close in Prayer**—Sing a worship song or two before closing in prayer. Invite members to pray that the Lord would overflow His love, grace and forgiveness in their marriages. Encourage them to pray aloud short sentence prayers of thanksgiving for God's love, perseverance, grace and reconciliation.

After the Meeting

1. **Evaluate**—Distribute the Study Review Forms for members to take home with them. Share about the importance of feedback, and ask members to take the time this week to write their review of the group meetings and then to return them to you.
2. **Encourage**—Call each couple during the next week and invite them to join you for the next study in the *Focus on the Family Marriage Series*.
3. **Equip**—Begin preparing and brainstorming new activities for the next Bible study.
4. **Pray**—Praise the Lord for the work He has done in the lives of the couples in the study. Continue to pray for these couples as they apply the lessons learned in the last few weeks.

Notes
1. Al Jansen, *The Marriage Masterpiece* (Wheaton, IL: Tyndale House Publishers, 2001).

Welcome to the Family!

As you participate in the *Focus on the Family Marriage Series*, it is our prayerful hope that God will deepen your understanding of His plan for marriage and that He will strengthen your marriage relationship.

This series is just one of the many helpful, insightful, and encouraging resources produced by Focus on the Family. In fact, that's what Focus on the Family is all about—providing inspiration, information, and biblically based advice to people in all stages of life.

It began in 1977 with the vision of one man, Dr. James Dobson, a licensed psychologist and author of 18 best-selling books on marriage, parenting, and family. Alarmed by the societal, political, and economic pressures that were threatening the existence of the American family, Dr. Dobson founded Focus on the Family with one employee and a once-a-week radio broadcast aired on only 36 stations.

Now an international organization, the ministry is dedicated to preserving Judeo-Christian values and strengthening and encouraging families through the life-changing message of Jesus Christ. Focus ministries reach families worldwide through 10 separate radio broadcasts, two television news features, 13 publications, 18 Web sites, and a steady series of books and award-winning films and videos for people of all ages and interests.

We'd love to hear from you!

For more information about the ministry, or if we can be of help to your family, simply write to Focus on the Family, Colorado Springs, CO 80995 or call 1-800-A-FAMILY (1-800-232-6459). Friends in Canada may write Focus on the Family, P.O. Box 9800, Stn. Terminal, Vancouver, B.C. V6B 4G3 or call 1-800-661-9800. Visit our Web site—www.family.org—to learn more about Focus on the Family or to find out if there is an associate office in your country.

Strengthen and enrich your marriage with these Focus on the Family® relationship builders.

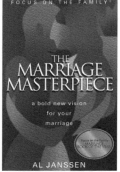

The Marriage Masterpiece
Now that you've discovered the richness to be had in "The Focus on the Family Marriage Series" Bible studies, be sure to read the book the series is based on. *The Marriage Masterpiece* takes a fresh appraisal of the exquisite design God has for a man and woman. Explaining the reasons why this union is meant to last a lifetime, it also shows how God's relationship with humanity is the model for marriage. Rediscover the beauty and worth of marriage in a new light with this thoughtful, creative book. A helpful study guide is included for group discussion. Hardcover.

The Love List
Marriage experts Drs. Les and Leslie Parrot present eight healthy habits that refresh, transform and restore the intimacy of your marriage relationship. Filled with practical suggestions, this book will help you make daily, weekly, monthly and yearly improvements in your marriage. Hardcover.

Capture His Heart/Capture Her Heart
Lysa TerKeurst has written two practical guides—one for wives and one for husbands—that will open your eyes to the needs, desires and longings of your spouse. These two books each offer eight essential criteria plus creative tips for winning and holding his or her heart. Paperback set.

• • •

STRENGTHEN MARRIAGES.
STRENGTHEN YOUR CHURCH.

Here's Everything You Need for a Dynamic Marriage Ministry!

Focus on the Family ® Marriage Series Group Starter Kit
Kit Box • Bible Study/Marriage • ISBN 08307.32365

Group Starter Kit includes:

• Seven Bible Studies: *The Masterpiece Marriage, The Passionate Marriage, The Fighting Marriage, The Model Marriage, The Surprising Marriage, The Giving Marriage* and *The Covenant Marriage*

• *The Focus on the Family Marriage Ministry Guide*

• *An Introduction to the Focus on the Family Marriage Series* video

Pick up the *Focus on the Family Marriage Series* where Christian books are sold.

Gospel Light